Goodnight Phone

by Beth Meese, RN
& William Morris, MD

illustrated by Ken Kula

Dedicated to my dearest wife, Keira, daughter Haley, and son, Holden....and of course my sad old phone.

— Will

Dedicated to my family and countless other families who need reminded of how beautiful life can be when you take a minute to look up from your phone.

— Beth

Good Night Phone - 1st edition. ISBN 978-0-692-76166-3
[1. Family-Fiction. 2. Phone-Fiction 3. Time-Fiction 4. Distraction-Fiction]
First Special Edition: December 2016. Printed in the United States. Printed on Recycled Paper.

My Phone's Name

_____

My Phone's Birthday
(date I got my phone)

_____

My Phone's Wake Time _____

My Phone's Bedtime _____

Good night my smart phone.

It's now time for bed.

We're done checking email.

All texts
have been read.

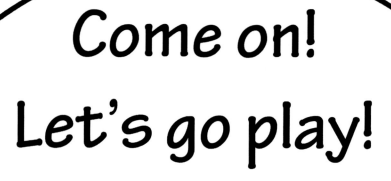

Please get ready
for bed,
your day is now done.

We're together all day, you buzz and you beep.

It's time to plug in,
go recharge;
get some sleep.

Put on your pajamas,
brush your teeth,
wash your face.

I will set your alarm
and hang up your case.

It's family time now,
not time for a phone;

...sharing stories
and building memories,
before we're all grown.

Grab your blanket,
bring your teddy.

Let's turn off your light.

We love you,
dear phone,
but it's time for
good night!

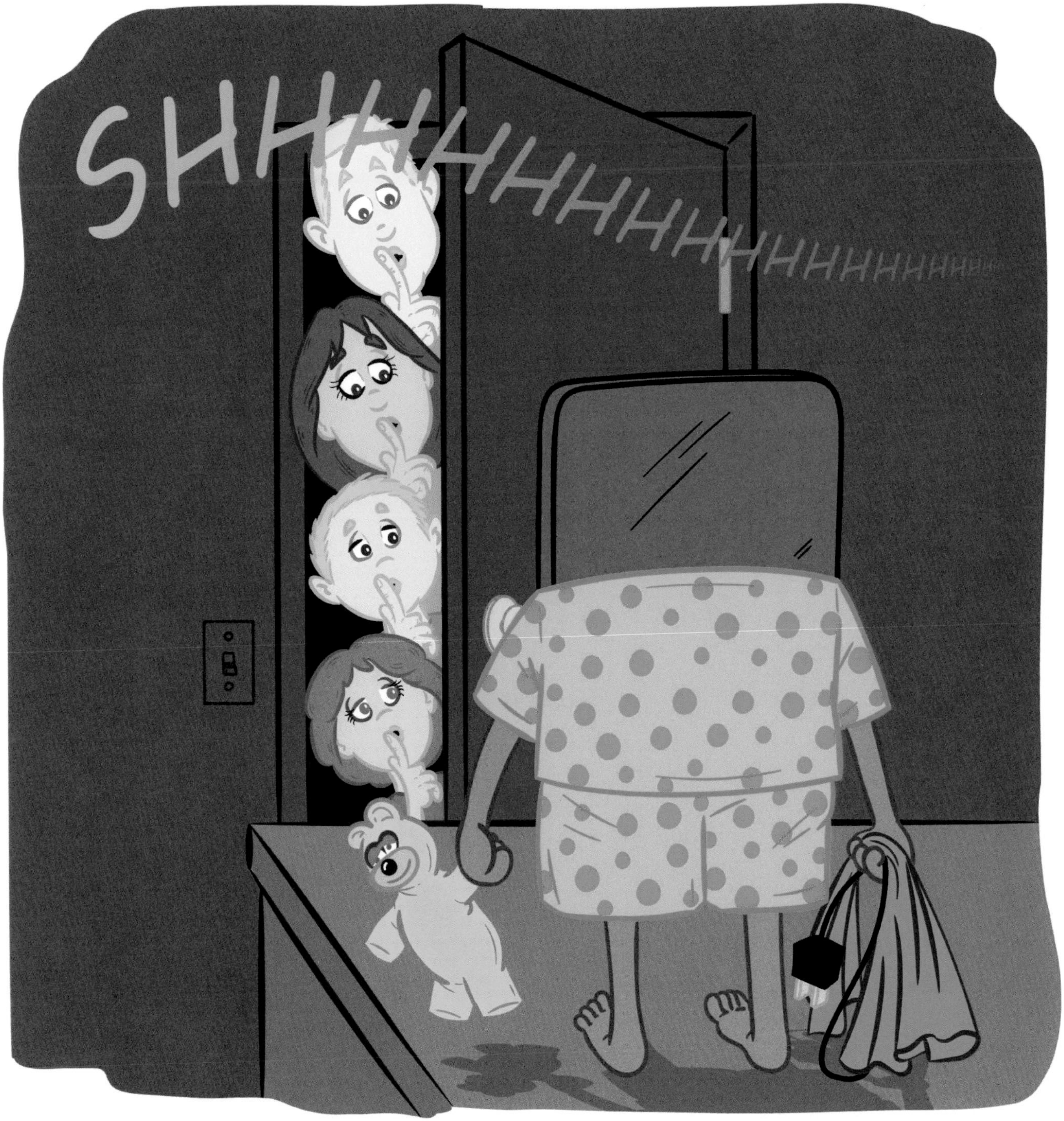
SHHHHHHHHHHHHHHHHHHHH

Climb into your bed
with a final *goodbye*.

Tomorrow will come
with a blink of an eye!

Sweet dreams,
see you in the morning!

They say the first step to any addiction is admitting you have a problem. I have a problem.
I am addicted to my phone. It wakes me up in the morning,
and I immediately check to see what I missed since I put it down the night before.
I am highly dependent on my phone for just about everything.

Our children are also growing up in this wired world.
My little one was not even 3 when she was playing an app one day and announced: "Battery dead."
Would I have even known what a device battery was when I was 3?
How did the excitement of something so useful turn into such a dependency?
What is this doing to our children and family structure?

Children model our behavior. Instead of "Do what I say, not what I do," they "do what we do."
We know that eliminating technology from our lives is not an option.
But at the same time, experts tell us that unstructured, unplugged play is the best way for young children
to learn to think creatively, to problem solve, and to develop reasoning, communication, and motor skills.
So can we find a balance to help our children and help ourselves?

There are simple things we can do to start. Remove the addictive devices from the room.
There is a time to check a device and a time to put them down. A text can wait. A post can wait.
A call can wait. The minutes we have with our children -- the priority and love they need -- cannot.

At the end of the day we cannot outpace technology, nor should we try to shut down technology or our
ever-growing desire to explore the depths of what technology and research can help us discover or uncover.
But we need to make good choices and send messages to our children. There is a simple way to start.
Give your phone a bedtime; put your phone to sleep.
Make a statement to your children that family time together is never substituted.

Good night phone

                   Beth Meese, RN

As a physician, husband, and a dad of two children, time is my
most coveted resource.
And sadly, every aspect of my life wants a piece of my time.
Over time I've come to rely upon my phone to help me manage.
But for me it is simple.
One day, my son said to me something that stopped me dead in
my tracks.

  "Dad, put your phone down and start living your life."

That's when I knew it was time for a change....Good night phone
                   Will Morris, MD

56915127R00020

Made in the USA
Columbia, SC
02 May 2019